Incognito

Tyler Neumann

Presentation by *BookLeaf Publishing*

Web: www.bookleafpub.com

E-mail: info@bookleafpub.com

ISBN: 9789358314540

First edition 2023

*I dedicate this collection of poems to the
creative Self in us all.*

ACKNOWLEDGEMENT

I want to acknowledge everyone who has ever truly seen me, and to all who wish to be seen.

PREFACE

This book of poetry is a gathering of messages I've pulled from within - from the serious, to the funny, to the seemingly mundane. It's the culmination of a small fraction of my inner thoughts that yearned to break free at this particular moment in time. What has been blocked for some time has broken through. I wrote these words as a promise to keep writing and letting creativity flow. The most important part of this book of poetry is not what's already inside, but what has yet to be written. It's a pact with myself that there is still so much more to share and that this is only a beginning. It's a pledge to no longer remain Incognito.

That Time

Universal change,
we all remember
That Time.

Shut in,
a world ill
in both body and soul.
Coming together,
retreating inside.
So much promise,
so much to unfurl.
The chance to heal,
to reach,
to listen.

Instead, division.
Worldwide promise…
Brushed off.
Thwarted.
Buried.
Horizon light,
dimmed and denied.
Facade of trust,
masked and ignored.
On the other side of it,

remnants of hope
even farther apart.
Lessons unlearned
and changed hearts
forgotten.

Physical realm
now partially healed.
How I yearn for a chance
to redo That Time,
so this virus of mind
could perhaps one day
be cured.

Where You Are From

That place you come from has a certain way
of doling out lie after lie.
Once trying to mold you into certain shapes,
a pattern you now dare defy.

The orderly, useless, and plain trickery
of the ones who wish you to stay:
"Stick to the plan of the way it should be."
Tricks be damned, if only halfway!

Set out on your own, fierce spirit you brought,
discovered the truth of true home.
First, imposter, uncomfortable thought,
then Master up high on your throne.

Ruler of paving the uncharted path
that is served up solely for some.
Decree and proclaim it, your life on behalf
of where you go, not where you are from.

Contradicting Emotions

Emptiness festers, thoughts undisclosed.
A life of enjoyment, juxtaposed.

Alone by the bay, idly still.
Joy creeping in, if only by pill.

Somber, downtrodden, under I sink.
Delight upon me, thanks to the drink.

Lower than low, unable to measure.
Somehow, some way, I muster up pleasure.

Clear as the night, something's amiss,
a grand fleeting moment encircled by bliss.

Awaiting and watching, feel thrown away,
elation upon me, naiveté.

Somber arousal, heart wide and vacant,
cheeriness feigns and leaves me complacent.

Funny how feelings exist all at once,
squeezing and pressing me down from all fronts.

Funny how feelings can bring harmony,
Yin and the Yang, all within me.

Unfold

Shut down, run out of town,
exploding into grace.
Overlooked and unheard,
unfolding at my pace.
Eyes seeking same eyes,
awed at the unseen.
Released from the chains
and feeling washed clean.
Quieting all worry,
entering the unknown.
Voice carried high,
a voice of my own.
What has been kept down low,
what has long been untold.
Releasing, rewarding,
a new life to unfold.

Every Haiku Has Its Season

Winter arrives first,
coldly biting all that lives
blanketing the Earth.

Spring sets in quickly,
proudly bursting through the soil,
all life on display.

Summer cocks its head,
sweetly bathing in the heat;
no rush to escape.

Fall leaves no traces,
softly taking us forward
to the next long year.

All seasons complete,
the cycle begins again.
Snow is on the way.

Greet the Sun

Sun rays stretch forward,
grounding all doubt.
Diagonal oranges and vertical yellows
meet divine reds center stage.
Mystical hues take root,
spreading seeds of hope,
shadows nary the wiser.
Ball of fire rising up,
darkness losing ground.
Neither steel nor stone dare hold it back.
The sky beckons to pull it in,
completely and fully.
Arms spread wide,
the blaze pierces through.
Light has won the day.

Silence

Do you hear it in the void?
Do you hear it in the breeze?
The stillness, the quiet, the joy.
The silence envelops, enwraps, and erupts,
and calls us to fall on our knees.

When will you accept it?
When will you enjoy?
When will you oblige the withdrawal of noise?

The clamor and banging of every day,
is no match for no voice and no sound.
The softness and peace,
will carry you home,
wherever the silence abounds.

A moment in time, is always enough,
to listen and stop silently.
Remember the reason,
the real noise that we crave,
is in doing it all quietly.

Gratitude

The tugging of Gratitude is felt within,
without it we'd cease to be.
Receiving the wonder and awe that has been,
allows us to live life carefree.

In knowing the good that the Universe provides,
energetically we fight for what's right.
Knowing that Gratitude is on our side,
the good will not leave from our sight.

It follows us, leads us to places unknown,
and dares us to never look back.
It hopes we will cherish the grace it has shown,
not focus on things that we lack.

When darkness and light seek an ominous fight,
it cheers us to side with the latter.
When threatened with changes from daytime to
night,
it pledges to shield all that matters.

Positive wishing, the theme for today,
no negatives, no no's, and no nots.
Just pluses and ups are coming your way
to transform and make over your thoughts.

Coffee

Coffee enjoyed with friends or alone,
the energy filling your cup.
Out of the ground, organically grown,
pulling you out of a slump.

In a French press or a batch of cold brew,
baristas will roast up the beans.
Customers waiting in long morning queues,
a part of their daily routines.

Espresso in tiny cups always delivered,
a boost to the Nth degree.
The caffeine hits hard, hands all in shivers,
one shot, or two shots, or three.

A café au lait filled up to the brim,
and lattes warmed up or on ice.
Milk choices prepped, be it whole, oat, or skim,
sweet syrups pumped once or pumped twice.

Several ways the coffee will flow,
poured over or casually dripped.
In porcelain mugs or concocted to-go,
a beverage globally sipped.

Training

The gym is a fun place to train and to sweat,
first stretching all of my muscles.
Mentally pushing away all regret,
with a session of HIIT in a hustle.

The workout continues, a set of EMOM,
then into a bout of AMRAP.
Striking my feet on the floor like a drum,
dumbbells heaved up in a snap.

Then off to a deadlift, heavy barbell,
so weighty and full of resistance.
My body will thank me when I'm on the scale,
displaying a lot of persistence.

Sometimes a bench press, a couple of rounds,
or a kettlebell swung high and low.
A race to prepare for, finish line bound,
my moment to put on a show.

Be it Marathon time or Spartan terrain,
I persevere until the end.
The pleasure I feel, I cannot explain,
the gym I do oft recommend.

So whether you're hesitant to join in the fun,
or wondering where to begin.
Just start with some movement, even just one,
your fitness and health, win-win.

Morning Commute

The rush and the hum of rubbery wheels,
sliding along the red lane.
Clickety-clack and bumpity-bump,
devouring all the terrain.

Screeching abruptly, the people descend,
door swung wide as a cave.
The driver is patient as I enter in,
accepting the nod that I gave.

The ride thrusting on as I move toward the back,
I'm eyeing which seat I should pick.
The bus so swift, starts to sway side to side,
my choosing has got to be quick.

Settling in to a seat with a view,
scanning in front and in behind.
Curious to know what brought others here,
our morning commute intertwined.

Before I know it, the ding of a bell,
not one second later requested.
Won't be long 'fore we stop again.
Looking 'round, all roads congested.

Repeating this way every block or two,
we're making headway on our journey.
Trying to find some peace before work,
praying no one will deter me.

Through red lights, tunnels, bridges, and hills,
not too much longer to go.
Done in a flash, yes, I've been here before,
it's Monday again, status quo.

The final long walk after my speedy exit,
the highway all in rearview.
Won't be much longer 'til I'm heading back,
and bidding my workplace adieu.

Graffiti

Since ancient times, those cave drawings chiseled,
stamps of an era long gone.
Pictures of past lives, obscurely scribbled,
for generations beyond.

Today is no different, the technique evolved,
new styles and wild fonts were designed.
Distinctive, suggestive, and rather involved,
it frequently goes undefined.

Plastered and painted on windows and walls,
sprayed into crevices deep.
Art of graffiti all over is scrawled,
murals embedded for keeps.

Private and public, the city is tagged,
marked with a personal touch.
Engraved and inscribed, illegally flagged,
with letters and symbols and such.

Some chalk it up to pure vandalism,
created to tarnish and taint.
Some are drawn in with a magnetism,
skilled craft so striking and quaint.

Subways and skyscrapers cannot compete,
they're merely just one more grand canvas.
No one can escape it, out in the streets,
the art meant to simply enchant us.

Golden Gate

In the Pacific, an entryway forms,
a port left wide open, ajar.
Beneath piers and wharfs, the seawater warms,
cruise ships advance from afar.
Captains of cargo shove off on sea swells,
coming and going with ease.
From worldly harbors, bidding farewell,
ushered by sea spray and breeze.
With scarlet-y tinge, a vast overpass,
agape and a beacon to fleets.
With minuscule sailboats below in contrast,
a prodigy of manmade feats.
Spanning expanses once unknown to man,
a red bridge is held in suspension.
The Golden Gate captivates, in strong command,
coaxing and drawing attention.
Whether hiking Land's End, with Cliff House in
view,
or sunbathing on Baker Beach,
giving respect where respect is due,
to the ruby platform within reach.
Fort Point to Marin, so ruggedly built,
travelers strolling in throngs.
Steady despite shaky earthquaking tilt,
port where the whole world belongs.

Dancing Fog

Through, around, and over the top,
circling over the city.
Yearly, daily, hourly. Nonstop.
Sun chased away, no pity.

Heaving itself on building and bone,
on valleys and hilltops alike.
Manifesting itself, no chaperone,
and living up to the hype.

Jiving above and prancing below,
shimmying down from the sky.
Unanchored haze with silvery glow,
waltzing to new lows and new highs.

Drabby and dreary, dull and subdued,
seemingly always adrift.
Strutting inward and in step from the sea,
always true to the script.

Seasons adjust, transform, and they shift,
petitioning for a chance.
Tangoing gently alongside the mist,
but the Fog insists on its dance.

Brazil

Surrounded by nature and sea,
paradise in reality.
Best thing in Búzios,
yummy and grandiose,
is a big bowl of Açaí.

Pão de queijo is great, too.
Brigadeiros through and through.
One day if I woke up,
a life Carioca,
Coxinhas, I'd eat beaucoup.

Amazon River, Manaus,
I went there once with my spouse.
Monkeys and gators,
below the Equator,
so happy I traveled down South.

The people show up often tarcy,
but Rio is clearly a party.
Copacabana and
Ipanema's white sand,
surfers on waves feeling gnarly.

Brazil in a nutshell, enthralled!

The colors and light, Carnival!
So happy to be there!
Amazing time, I swear!
The charm and the bliss you'll recall!

Noble Thing

Acceptance is a noble thing,
requiring fear and courage and trust.
Hinges break free, doors open within,
deciding this is a must.

Acceptance is a noble thing,
requiring hope and faith and light.
The lock is the key to what's been closed in,
new thoughts and new days to ignite.

Acceptance is a noble thing,
requiring pain and love and heart.
Someone said to me, I don't know when,
this moment will be a fresh start.

Acceptance is a noble thing,
requiring joy and effort and time.
I do believe, and with a smile,
the result will be sublime.

If Love Is

If love is kind and gentle and unwavering;
If love is wanting and waiting from dusk to
dawn;
If love is thoughts and hopes of what may be;
If love is found in a moment's look,
a simple touch,
a heartfelt grin;
If love has an explanation yet goes unexplained;
If love is calm and easy and wonderful;
Then one thing I know is certain...
I undoubtedly love you.

Nature

Nature sweeps us forward and inward and
deeper.
It calms and strikes the soul
with fierce waves of knowing and
understanding.
Nature pulls out of us what stays in.
It carries, and lifts, and moves
in vibrations that sweeten and soothe.
Nature urges, no, requires
that we listen, release, and open fully.
It wanders and winds toward nothing and
everything simultaneously.
Nature flows and is free and begs us to follow.
It know what to say when we are left speechless.
Nature runs through our veins with breathtaking
beats.
It cleanses and creates when our canvas is dry.
Nature readies us and ripens our being where the
unnatural rots.
It says to us, "Come, Be Still, and Wonder What
Could Be."
Nature guides and leads a mysterious journey,
and because of this...
It is part of you and me.

Ravens' Flight

Horizon Sun setting, the Ravens appear,
gliding in simple formation.
Window light captures them, both far and near,
nightly celestial migration.

Off in the night and succumbing to dark,
flocking in Conspiracy.
Diving and fluttering off on a lark,
hovering in Treachery.

Whirling and twirling, as if in a Rave,
belting out one last long shriek.
Delicate flapping of wings in a wave,
surely toward midnight sleep.

Daylight awakens, and coffee is poured,
the Ravens returning to flight.
Reversing direction this early morn,
slowly retreating from sight.

Where do they come from, and where do they
go,
wandering all through the day?
Swooping and squawking in flight to and fro,
circling over the Bay.

Out chasing seagulls or perched on a ledge,
with sharp bird's eye view scanning down.
Perhaps, nestled on neighboring hedge,
then out to the next one crosstown.

Wherever they end up, no one is spared,
from the shadowy beauty airborne.
The Ravens' great flight, no nothing compares,
to its elegance daily reborn.

It's Time

Rise up, jump in, and achieve it, my friend.
Time now to flourish, beginning to end.

The moment has come to reshape your fate.
Now's not too early, nor is it too late.

Be steadfast and clear and want what is true.
Know yourself closely in all that you do.

Through time and space, seize life on a whim.
Gaze up in the sky, allow Jupiter in.

Run up that hill, friend, not once looking back.
Speed up, look forward, you're on the right
track.

Each hurdle, and step, and leap on the trek,
the cosmos behind you, all hands on deck.

Hang on, grab life, put your mind to the grind.
And remind yourself often…"It's Time! It's
Time!"

All Grown Up

Early days playtime, young and carefree,
best friends in the blink of an eye.
Imagining dragons, parading with glee,
arms spreading widely to fly.

Badminton, baseball, and biking the town,
scrambling onto the trees.
Sunbathing, sleepovers, snooping around,
fresh games of hide and go seek.

Teen time goes turbulent, tough to intake,
clashing and conflict abound.
Awareness is heightened, oh what to make,
of adolescent breakdown.

Taking on more of what life has to gift,
maturing and coming of age.
Nowhere near ready to manage the shift,
teen years are turning the page.

Adulthood affirms what we never did learn,
thrown into the world on our own.
Answer to no one, always concerned,
anxiety swelling, full-blown.

All grown up, and heaven forbid,
we retrace the steps of our youth.
Forgetting, refusing, to act like a kid,
because we have something to prove.

Pretending is present when young and when old,
the difference is found in the theme.
A life that was once rather uncontrolled,
as adults we fall prey to the scheme.

Advice for the wise, live life free and wild,
you're worth it, you silly goose!
Do not deny the inner young child,
the growth in your life no excuse!